"In her book, *Grief F*
beautifully descripti
how people experier
a very real and com
offers excellent practical suggestions that are amazingly helpful in coming
to a "brighter beyond." Lynn's book is a must-read for those who are per-
sonally experiencing the road of grief, for friends and work colleagues, and
for seasoned clinicians who are helping people walk their journey."

- Bob Colclough, MA, LPC

"Lynn Robinson's writing affirms that both love and grief are sent from the
heart to the brain. Her book is beautifully put together and is well-written."

- Morris Weiss, MD

"I could not put the book down! I appreciate the varied experiences fea-
tured because they offer hope, clarity, inclusion, and patience with self.
I'm reminded that when someone you love has died, grief fog arrives in
surprising moments whether earlier or later or both. I love this book. So
helpful."

- Sherril Arnold, RN

"Using real-life examples, Lynn Robinson has written a well-thought out
book about grief experiences. As she discusses, grief fog is something not
commonly talked about but is an authentic symptom of grieving. All of us
have had to deal with different forms of grief; this book also gives us very
effective tools and treatment options to help the healing process, which in
turn helps treat the brain fog."

- Chris Brown, MD

GRIEF FOG

And a Brighter Beyond

Lynn B. Robinson, Ph.D.

atmosphere press

Published by Atmosphere Press

ISBN 979-8-89132-567-8

Cover design by Matthew Fielder

Atmospherepress.com

Table of Contents

Introduction

Death is inescapable; life is finite. I know that.

Until my husband's unexpected death, I had not known grief would bring misty, brain-saturating clouds. I did not know that grief would cripple my thinking and envelop my mind in a fog.

As days and weeks went by, I hoped and looked for a way out of the fog. Having been a college professor, a business consultant, and an author, I leaned into memory and experience.

I sat at my desk, staring at my computer. I read about grief. During daytime naps or night time sleep, I sometimes had dreams about escaping the fog.

At some point, I don't remember when, the idea for this book emerged. Because I knew that both academic studies and personal stories had been written about grief, I was hesitant to write another.

Talking to friends about their grief did two things. It gave me hope for brighter days and lessened my hesitancy to write.

Now, I share that hope with you.

For each of us, for family and friends, there is a path away from fog. The distance of the path may differ. The choice to take it is individual.

Perhaps this book will be your compass. I wish you well.

PART ONE

EXPERIENCING A LOVED ONE'S DEATH

Alive ... then Not

Where did you go? You were just here. I could touch you. Looking at your face, your body, if I leaned in close, I could hear your breathing.

And then your breathing stopped.

I can still see and touch your body, but you are no longer there.

How did that happen?

Where are you? Or are you *you* at all?

The uncertainty catches in my throat. I feel myself gasping for breath. From somewhere I hear and feel racking sobs...and realize they are mine.

Gradually I begin to wonder who I am, if I will ever feel like I did just yesterday. I have a difficult time remembering who I was before I had become not just me but "we" with you.

As days, weeks, and months go slowly by, I realize there must be answers. The answers, I surmise, may differ. Death is inescapable, and others may be willing to help me find my way without you ... to share their paths from we to me.

And so, I begin asking ... and sharing ... to help me understand ... and to help you, too.

You are reading. You care. I'm glad, less sad.

Thank you.

Lynn

Life goes on ... I forget just why.
- Edna St. Vincent Millay

As I begin writing my story, it has been 370 days since my husband's death. It feels like forever and yesterday. If that sounds confused, it is because I feel that way. And sometimes, perhaps too often, I think that way.

On a Friday, late afternoon, Robbie came home earlier than usual, not by much but a little. He headed for the bedroom, his facial expression and body posture expressing discomfort.

I went to him as he prepared to lie down and stopped him to help him unbuckle his belt and step out of his trousers. As I pulled back the covers, he got into bed but failed to put on the mask for his CPAP machine he'd been using for years to facilitate easy breathing. I reached for the mask and helped him put it on.

My concern for his well-being was on high alert. During his 81 years, illness had been rare. I sat in the lounge chair in our bedroom to be nearby should he need me.

After about a half-hour, he sat up, removed the C-pap mask, stood up and began walking toward, I thought, his "man cave," where he enjoyed reading on his home computer at his desk. But he had not said a word. I quickly followed him and saw that he had seated himself in our den-like living room, a room away from his desk.

His body posture told me he still did not feel at all well. I felt his forehead and left him to get a thermometer. His temperature was about 101. I fixed an ice pack to hold to his head and offered to get an aspirin. He refused. I said I wanted to call 911. He said "No." I called our son who lives close by to tell him his dad was not well and to please be available; he told me he and his wife weren't at home, but about twenty minutes away. I called our daughter who was many hundreds of miles away to tell her I was concerned ... which in retrospect was somewhat irrational, or maybe it was intuitive.

My husband continued to look distressed. I asked again about calling 911 for help. Again, he refused. Another five minutes or so went by, I asked again to call 911, and my husband agreed. I made that call and then immediately called our son.

The 911 emergency crew arrived, came inside and determined quickly to put my husband on a stretcher, take him to their rescue vehicle, and then to our preferred hospital (one that had his records from minor surgery some years prior). My son arrived in time to follow them to the hospital. I called my daughter to tell her...she flew in the next day.

The following morning, Saturday, and again on Sunday, my husband was remarkably better though still in intensive care at the hospital. We awaited the results of assorted tests and visits from physicians. On Monday morning, he had taken a turn for the worse and was in perilous condition, his heart seriously weakened. He died that night: February 6. Our sixtieth wedding anniversary would have been three weeks later, February 27.

I know that my children and I called the crematory; we went there to make arrangements. I have the papers but remember none of the details. I know we called our church and met with our senior pastor in his office to plan a funeral and to do whatever else he recommended. I know that friends and neighbors quickly learned of my husband's death and began bringing food, doing errands, and in other ways letting us know they cared deeply. I recall very few details. Perhaps I will in the future; I'll know when I know.

I guess I mechanically did the things I had to do...eat, sleep, dress, go places, write thank you notes to so many people who showered me with kindnesses. I began remembering a little and enjoying a few things. And, then, very early in the morning of July 20, my older sister died. She had been ill for a long time; I was pleased for her that she had been released from her discomfort. Even so, I grieved deeply; I had never known life without her.

Intense grief fog slowly re-entered and moved through my brain. My need to keep a calendar, to make written reminders, became paramount. I told myself that my problem was my age: 85; I lied.

Five months after my sister's death, in December, one of my closest lifelong friends died, followed a few weeks later by one of my older brother's who had been like another big brother to me when I was little. A new wave of grief brain's fog crept in. Given that I am in my mid-eighties, either I'll die or continue to somewhat regularly tell others good-bye. Will the fog ever lift? Grief-brain diminish?

My life had been one of accomplishment. I began setting small goals...things beyond getting up and dressed, provisioning my home, and paying bills. Inside of the fog, I knew that wasn't enough. I needed to assess and give recognition to the everyday wonders of life.

I have neighbors who have continued a tradition we began several years earlier during the Covid shut-down; we gather in my driveway most evenings for about an hour. I have returned to a weekly Bible class. I go routinely for physical therapy and more...those kinds of regular things one does and those things that may reopen or reconstruct some sense of normality.

Someone told me...or I read somewhere...that year two is often harder than the first. In the first, you have so much legal and other stuff to do. Then, in the second, with less of that, the loss can hit really hard. A few days ago, in the morning, I stood in my husband's mostly empty closet and sobbed. I had had a good night's sleep, better than many...but I lay down on the bed and fell asleep for at least an hour. Got up, did a few house-type things, and had a light lunch. A short time later, for a second time, I burst into prolonged tears. Got back in the bed and fell asleep again! Eventually got up...don't remember what I did until it was time to join some friends for about an hour. Supper and evening were pretty much routine. I went to bed as usual with no difficulty falling asleep. Inexplicable.

Maybe crying is one way we bathe from the inside out...a way we wash out the grief a tiny bit at a time.

In writing to a recently widowed friend about the day of tears and naps, she commiserated, "I have trouble reading books about grief. I always end up crying, and music is not my friend either. It helps to know others are feeling the same pain." And she told me about a mutual friend who has expressed similar thoughts about the second year being more difficult, saying, "I worked for a couple of months after Jim died and probably shouldn't have because of the brain fog." She, too, is still grieving.

When I think about my husband, I remember his many business, civic, and personal endeavors. I smile at some, cry about others, sometimes laugh, am occasionally angry, and often feel very alone. I realize I continue to scurry back and forth in random order among the stages of grief: Denial and Isolation, Anger, Bargaining, Depression, and Acceptance, as introduced by Elizabeth Kubler-Ross, MD, in her 1969 hugely influential book, *On Death and Dying,* where she also describes hope jumping about among those stages as one accepts the inevitability. Even with the sense-pounding reality of my husband's death, the daily, hourly, minute-by-minute knowing he is not physically here and will never be again...I hold onto hope.

My hope is twofold: that I can and shall fully enjoy being with living family and friends. And that I'll remember, that I'll break through the fog of grief.

A third hope is that I'll be able to communicate more fully with friends and loved ones no longer in their physical bodies. I've done so for most of my life and have previously published two books about that. Even those mediumistic communications have diminished with grief-fog. Have I heard from my husband since he left his body? Yes. Do I wish for more? Yes, and I yearn for it to be more physical, knowing it cannot.

I remind myself that I am loved, lovable and loving. I look forward to believing.

Amy

The important thing is to strive towards a goal which is not immediately visible.
That goal is not the concern of the mind, but of the spirit.
- Antoine de Saint-Exupery

Virginia had been sick for several years. A lengthy illness caused her general health and her mobility to become increasingly limited. The final time she was admitted to the hospital, her daughters were bedside with her. With her demise obvious, Virginia requested hospice. The nursing staff discontinued all medication. Virginia's discomfort turned to misery, to hours of agony. Hospice care had been inexplicably delayed.

Her daughter, Amy, recalled becoming anxious. "It wasn't supposed to be that way. With hospice, we anticipated her death would be seamless: easy, with no pain," she told me. When finally hospice provided pain-reduction assistance, Virginia became calm and occasionally spoke. Her eyes closed, Virginia whispered to her daughters, "The bluebirds are coming to get me. The dogs are all here." Remembering the family's many pet dogs brought slight smiles to her daughters.

Amy heard her mom's last breath. "It was deep and then a sigh. For at least twenty-four hours, everything seemed surreal," she said. "I couldn't take time to grieve completely," she continued. "I had to take care of Daddy." Amy's tears made talking difficult. "When you lose your mom, your world just changes. I postponed my grief. When my dad died, I had a double dose."

There were more tears before Amy spoke again. "When Mom died, everything changed. It was a devastating loss; we were so close. The whole day of the funeral was like being in a dream." Another pause, more tears. "There were so many

11

people. It was amazing, such a tribute for such a beautiful, beautiful person."

Amy and I talked a little about the demands on her time and her energy. "I really relate to the term brain-fog," she said. "I couldn't keep a thought. I couldn't concentrate. It was weird. I could barely form a sentence. I had to get a sedative to be able to sleep. I was so stressed out. But I had to work, to keep my job." Taking a deep breath, she continued, "I could hardly function. I couldn't stay focused on a task. I was easily distracted; it was weird!"

Then, referring to her father's death three years later, Amy said that she cried off and on a lot. "I had to make so many decisions, big ones, like deciding what to do with their house." She paused, then continued, "My sister and I talked often. You know, she lives two states away and has responsibilities there. She told me she felt bad about not being able to come here more frequently. Talking helped."

Following another brief pause, Amy said, "I remember feeling completely exhausted. I could not concentrate. There was such a void."

We both took deep breaths. Softly, I asked Amy if she could remember anything that had helped lessen her sadness. Amy's eyes brightened, and she smiled. "When Mom was in the hospital, before we asked for hospice, the TV was on. We were watching together: Sex and the City." Her smile lessened, a touch of sadness returning. "As we watched, Mom said, 'I'm never going to be able to wear a pretty dress like that again.' And then she said she'd never see Daddy again."

I was silent, letting Amy collect her thoughts.

"I had grief fog for months. And then again with Daddy. It's so final with no parents! When grief fog would envelop me, I could not concentrate and sometimes felt I was unable to put one foot after another."

With her mother's and father's illnesses, Amy's sister came whenever she could. "It was always hard when she drove away," she said. "We would both cry. It was always hard telling her goodbye."

"I still have intermittent grief," she said. "And I cry. I miss them. I talk to them, to their pictures. Sometimes, I see bluebirds and cardinals. That makes me feel like they're nearby." And she added, "Shortly after Mom's death, I felt someone sit on my bed."

Amy was able to tell me about a couple of things that have helped her: time and being busy with work. She's been able to grow her business which she suggested has kept her from dwelling on her loss. "And my dog Pearl helped immensely," Amy said. "She was my best friend through it all." Even so, Amy says, "I think I'm still grieving."

I asked Amy for a vivid memory of her mom. "Hearing her voice. And growing up, I'd hear her high heels coming across the front porch and think 'Momma's home'!" "Even now," she added, "sometimes I think we smell her —the perfume she always wore." Amy paused before adding, "Another fond memory is sitting with her and having long heart-to-heart talks, maybe with hot tea and sometimes wine, depending on whether it was cocktail hour. And she always had great advice."

Amy's big beautiful smile brightened her face. "She used to tell me she was so proud of me."

Her mother has been gone for ten years, and her dad for seven.

"I thank God every night for Mom and Daddy. We were so blessed, such a loving and stable family. My childhood was idyllic. We didn't have the biggest house or the most of anything, but I had everything I needed."

Kay

What Bill and Kay had anticipated would be a routine doctor visit was not. Though Bill had a series of illnesses for 22 years, neither was prepared to hear the doctor say, "Bill has leukemia; it is terminal." Kay began crying. "You can expect about three to five months of life without treatment, or fifteen to eighteen months with treatment."

Kay continued crying and could not stop. "When I heard the word terminal, my crying was immediate," she said.

"I had dealt with death before. It was so different. When I was sixteen, my mother died. She was playing the organ when the song abruptly stopped; my mother was dead. I was in shock. I didn't cry. Many friends came to the house. My father and siblings left everything to me; I entertained. I went away to college. The first time I came home during my freshman year, everything was just so different. I shut down completely. I did not menstruate for the whole year." She paused, laughed softly, and commented about being glad she'd not been sexually active because she would have added to the stress of her loss.

Kay continued, "I'd been away from home before for life studies, for camp, for other things. It wasn't being away from home. I stayed shut-down emotionally through college. I could have and did have fun. Others probably didn't know. I never cried. I just did not...until my forties. Then I grieved and cried for my mother."

When I asked why she began crying then, Kay was hesitant to answer. She didn't want to remember, to divulge. Ultimately, quietly, she shared concerns about some poor

14

behavioral choices made by their children, problems that were typical of the time period but had triggered Kay's delayed crying for her mother.

Because of that earlier emotional breakthrough, when she and Bill were told of his terminal diagnosis, her tears flowed. She started grieving immediately. In the twenty months after Bill's diagnosis, Kay experienced intermittent grieving. Her grief heightened when Bill could no longer do things he had always done. As an example, she recalled that they had needed a tree cut down. Bill had called professionals. "Usually," Kay told me, "Bill would have gone outside, talked to the men, and enjoyed the process. He loved things like that. But he didn't get out of his chair." Because of that, Kay said she cried and couldn't stop. Her grief was triggered by things he couldn't do.

Ultimately, Bill went to a hospice facility. Kay and their children were faithful in their attention and care. He had told all of them that he did not want them with him at the actual time of death. "When it's time," he said, "go get some coffee." On the Monday evening of his death, they left at 7 p.m. Arriving home, they received the call. Bill had died just after they left. They went back, staying with him for about two hours.

Our conversation paused briefly. I asked Kay what the next 24 hours had been like. "Even after anticipating his death, it was like being stunned that he was really gone."

"And what about now?" I asked. Without hesitation, Kay told me, "Life has changed drastically. I've had to get used to being by myself. For me, it's an unusual way to live. I come from a family of seven and was married right out of college. It's just very usual. It turns out there were so many things I didn't know and don't know how to do. Bill fixed everything. I didn't know how to buy a light bulb." She paused. "I can't say I'm depressed. I started grieving when the physician said 'terminal'. I've been able to grieve all along, grieve and be ok with grief. I knew from my twenties how detrimental every-thing was...my wanting to be brave then. Now I know that 'bravery' isn't necessary; I have no problem grieving." Pausing, Kay looked beyond me. She continued, "I'm a people person, but since he died, I've just wanted to stay home. I have a fear of going out, of being around people, of being triggered and starting to cry."

Kay understood the term grief fog immediately. She thinks it needs to be taken seriously because of the behavioral changes that accompany it. She described how her driving had been affected in the first fourteen days after Bill's death. On two different occasions, she pulled into traffic from a side street into a busier one. Each time, she braked and then accel-erated, did so again, and continued jerkily while cars behind her honked impatiently. "I've never had a wreck," she told me. "That was frightening." Fortunately, it hasn't happened again.

There were other ways grief fog manifested for Kay. She would feel overwhelmed and couldn't make decisions. "The first month was really bad," she said. "If the least little thing would go wrong, I'd just go to pieces. When Bill was alive, there was never any stress if something broke. He could fix anything." She chuckled softly, "Since his death, I've realized he had an unbelievable amount of tools."

I asked her if she had sensed Bill in any way since his death. "In our bedroom I've sensed him twice. There was no message. I didn't see anything."

"But before he died, there was something. It was the night of his terminal diagnosis. I was in such grief. My crying stopped. I turned on the TV, and in my peripheral vision, I saw three beings. Then I looked squarely at them, and they stayed there. They were dark, but I could see them: a head, shoulders, and then they went straight to the floor. I was not afraid of them."

I remarked, "If you were not afraid, perhaps they were angels."

Kay tilted her head, then spoke directly to me, "Maybe," she said, "but I remember thinking that I was seeing his deceased grandmother, mother, and sister." Kay paused. "The losses I experienced with my mother and with Bill were so different. With my mother, there was a lengthy depression without tears. With Bill, I cried from the beginning, but I'm not depressed; I'm sad."

She paused again. Grief fog for Kay included fear. "I had to take over his business. I was totally overwhelmed. Now I have a handle. But grief caused me not to think straight."

"My grief is diminished but ongoing," Kay confided. "There can just be something small, and I'll start crying. But I may be beyond grief fog."

Friends have helped Kay. Other widows invited her to visit, saying, "You probably won't want to come, but you need to make yourself come." Kay says they were right about that.

People from her church have kept up with Kay: "They've made a difference."

"And my children have been unbelievable." I could hear the love in her voice. Then she told me of their new family tradition. They eat out every Thursday evening. "That's tightened us up. Made us stronger. Is important," she concluded.

Joan

The virtue of the candle lies not in the wax that leaves its trace but in its light.
- Antoine de Saint-Exupery

Losing someone you love requires great strength. Perhaps the shorter time you have for in-person love, the more difficult it can be. When I called somewhat hesitantly asking Joan if she would talk to me, her answer without hesitation: "Yes." Her willingness to discuss the death of her three-month-old granddaughter, Carrie, is a gift. Joan told me then, "Until you feel grief, you don't know how strong love can be."

For the most part, life was returning to normal for Hannah and Will. Each would again be going to work; their older daughter, Jenny, on that day to grandmother Joan's; and the baby, Carrie, to infant-care. The day began normally and ended tragically. Under unusual circumstances, without warning, three-month-old Carrie died that day.

Immediately following and for days afterward, Joan recalled, there was "a feeling of circling the wagons, of family being close." Joan described other family members who live close by gathering together quickly and Hannah's parents who came in from another city joining them later that night. "There was such a feeling of love; it was overwhelming."

The family was so intent on being together, supporting each other, that they had spoken to no one, except, of course the professionals who must be called for necessary services. That must have been more than enough for word of Carrie's death to spread. "The next morning," Joan recalled, "friends arrived at our house—friends who had experienced tragedies in their own lives. I remember thinking that if they knew, everyone knows, though I still don't know how." She paused, smiling a little. "The fact that everyone knew made it so much

18

easier. And it was like the whole community wrapped their arms around us. That helped so much."

For several days, the family lived in very close contact. "We talked a lot. We prayed a lot. We understood that God knows our lives, that He feels our heartbreak. He wants the best for us and will care for us through it. His love for us was and is evident in our friends' eyes, kind words, and actions. He made Hannah and Will special; their support for each other is inspirational." She added, "And they have a really tight network of friends who, for weeks, gathered together nightly with them."

Joan smiled, eyes twinkling, "From the beginning, we had people surrounding us. The Holy Spirit was with us."

Talking with Joan was a little like playing hop-scotch. Our conversation jumped about a bit. I had the sense that so did her feelings. And mine began doing the same.

"After Carrie's death," Joan continued, "I immediately felt empathy for other people. I suddenly realized we are a community. I could feel a connection with other people's pain."

I asked her if she had experienced grief fog. "I'm not sure I've really felt that. I felt anxiety. I felt like I needed to stay strong for the family, especially for my husband. Because he thinks of himself as the patriarch of our family, he thought he should be able to hold it all together for everyone. I knew I needed to be strong for him, for our children and grandchildren."

It has been 16 months since Carrie died. Her father says his grief fog may have begun lessening. Others in the family may have and may continue to experience grief fog. Joan mentioned her husband as possibly being among those. With a hint of laughter, she said, "And this tragedy has magnified aging changes for us both."

"Are you doing anything to help you get through this?" I inquired.

Joan told me that writing to people for their gifts, cards, and letters was helpful, that it was like talking to friends. "As time went by, I'd write to them again. I did this for months and wrote maybe a hundred or more letters." With hardly a pause, she added, "My faith helped. The Lord wants us to be happy." An even briefer pause. "I chose to go to counseling. And my other grandchildren help."

"Is there something you vividly remember about Carrie?" I asked.

"She was beginning to coo and to smile. She had dark curly hair which was unusual for our family. And, she was beginning to be her own person," Joan added.

"I think," Joan continued, "that God is heart-broken for us. He wants us to be happy, and He works for our best interest, helping us."

"Joan," I asked, "do you think you've been in contact in any way with Carrie?"

She smiled and told me, "I had two dreams not long after she died. In the first one, I was sitting with a group of friends showing them pictures of her. In the second dream, our family was at the beach where Hannah casually told me she was looking for Carrie, and I told her, 'Oh, I can help you. Aunt Sue has her, and she's fine.' I can remember a feeling of relief in my dream. Aunt Sue was known in our family as being very loving; she's been dead for three or so years. And, she really believed that, following the deaths of her own parents, they had come back to see her many, many times."

"Are there other things that are especially meaningful to you?" I asked.

"The way the other seven children in the family have reacted," she said. "Immediately after Carrie's death, our children and grandchildren were at our house all the time. We have a box full of sticky alphabet letters; one of the grand-daughters would take all of the letters that were Carrie's initials and stick them all over her face and tell us 'I'm doing this to remember Carrie.' As a group, they'd pick flowers in our yard and float them in the swimming pool, saying, 'This is for Carrie.' When her two-year-old sister returned to day care, she'd go off by herself and whisper. 'What are you doing?' her teacher would ask. 'I'm talking to Carrie.'" As I write this, I can't remember if Joan and I smiled, laughed, cried or did all three. Probably all three.

Joan spoke first. "We're changed. We're all changed. I'm a completely different person, and so is my husband. I think it helps to talk about it. I feel like it's life. In our humanity we're sharing. Death is a part of life." Another brief pause before she continued, "My worry and concern for my son is greater for me than the grief for my grandchild." Another pause. "The impact of her death, though, is monumental and shows the power of love." Another pause. "We had her only three months."

Joan's sadness showed in her facial expression. "My son's grief has impacted me so much. You're only as happy as your most unhappy child."

We were quiet for a few moments. Suddenly Joan smiled broadly and said, "Aunt Sue, the one keeping Carrie, loved unconditionally...no tough love, just love. I rarely remember dreams, but I remember the two I told you about. I know the Lord and Aunt Sue have Carrie, so she's fine. I'll never forget that dream, for sure."

Then her smile began fading, and I felt I needed to say something...maybe not the best thing: "Wherever there's loss, there's hurt."

Smiling again, Joan said, "That's because there was love first."

Alan

Even our misfortunes are part of our belongings.
- Antoine de Saint-Exupery

Mary had not been feeling herself for several years; confusion and memory lapses occurred and slowly increased with time. Thirteen years before her death, her disease was diagnosed. It progressed slowly, with Alan able to care for Mary at home until her deteriorating condition demanded change. She needed more professional care in the final months leading to her inevitable death.

When I asked Alan about his state of being in the 24 hours prior to Mary's death, he did not hesitate. "I was in a form of shock, knowing minute by minute, each could be her last, but I still was not prepared. I was almost like a zombie, knowing she was going. Though I knew it was coming and had years to prepare, I was still not prepared."

In the immediate hours after her death, even having known it was inevitable, Alan recalled being on "automatic pilot." He began thinking about logistics, about the things that had to be done. Because her death was during the height of Covid shut-downs, which began in March 2020, he knew the logistics would be difficult. Pausing momentarily, he explained an earlier decision by both of them was to have their bodies donated for research. Because that had already been decided, he remembered feeling he didn't have to worry.

Decision making suddenly occurred without forethought. Alan recalled he just started doing things...almost as though death had not occurred. "I felt sort of out of-body," he recalled. "I felt little emotion. Covid complicated things. Everyone had to wear masks. All of the things I knew I must do, I just did, not fretfully...in an automatic way."

He paused, then continued, "As days went by, I started feeling sick, like I wanted to go to bed and pull up the covers....disappear under them. But I knew that was out of the question."

Sometime in those first days or weeks after Mary's death, a friend joined Alan and some others. "He's a charming man, and we've been friends a long time. He's a great storyteller. He started talking, telling stories about life, ones I'd heard him tell before. I became really annoyed. I didn't want to hear stories I knew really well. I told the group, 'I need to go home to bed.' My annoyance sort of surprised me. I was stunned. Though people will tell you that you'll feel just fine, I didn't feel just fine. It's a many-layered experience."

"My life had begun changing in profound ways. When Mary began having seizures, she needed the assistance of professionals in a skilled care facility. Every day, I would be there to feed her lunch and supper; she was unable to feed herself. When I was in her presence, I felt peace and purpose. After feeding her supper, I'd get her ready for bed and watch her drift off to sleep. That was not hard. When I was with her, I had perfect peace."

Alan hesitated and then continued, "When she was gone, peace and purpose left. That was really hard. I know she's in a better place, but she was absent from me. That was really rough and continued for a good while."

I asked Alan if, during that time, he had experienced what might be called grief-brain or grief fog. "Grief fog, I definitely was in a fog, sometimes a dense fog."

Alan again mentioned the length of Mary's illness. The early years when she still lived at home had allowed them to maintain some semblance of normality. But her disease took a big step down and then another. During those ending years, the only time he felt a deep loneliness, a pain, as though he were sick, was at the dinner table at Thanksgiving and Christmas, but "I covered it up," he told me. He contrasted that with those same holidays in the first two years after Mary's death, saying, "Those were awful!" He hesitated, then told me something had changed. "The third Christmas after Mary's death was the happiest I had in sixteen years. It was a great delight seeing things through my grandchildren's eyes."

I asked Alan if he could identify something that helped him move away from his intense grief. "Friends who had lost spouses formed a group. We met for about eighteen months. It was helpful to talk about it. I discovered that most people don't want you to talk about the death of a loved one. At first they're good about it, but after a while it makes them uncomfortable. In the group, we all wanted to talk, and we all wanted to listen." He paused. "You know, our culture is not comfortable with grieving."

Alan hesitated again and looked as though he was deep in thought. "Grief has a life of its own," he continued. "It has to flow. It changes on its own."

I saw the opportunity to ask Alan about things that may have helped him manage his grief. "What surprised you that helped?" I asked.

His eyes twinkled. "Mary and I had traveled often with one couple. After her death, I often had dinner with them. Each time, they'd have a picture from a different trip together. I couldn't have foreseen pulling out a photograph would help. It was comforting at a deep level."

Again, he hesitated. "Another thing that helped me was something a physician friend told me. He said I should turn on all the lights in my house in the afternoon and evenings. And it helped! It made a difference!" Another pause, and then he continued, "I had a neighbor who would not leave her house after her husband's death. Her health diminished. Her physician prescribed sunshine, telling her she needed to sit in the sunshine for thirty minutes every day. She followed his instructions, and within three months she began leaving her house."

Alan hesitated before saying, "My sister reminded me to do that. It made a difference." He commented that the sun prescription had been appropriate for diminishing his grief fog. "It's simple things that can help reduce that fog...just being able to talk. It's a gift to let the person talk. Don't interrupt; allow him to talk. You have no obligation to say comforting words. Your gift is to listen."

"I still have grief fog," he continued. "But I'm in a very different place. It still comes, not as ferociously or frequently. Sometimes now talking about Mary brings a smile instead of a tear."

Alan hesitated. His tone of voice changed. "You can't expect your children to grieve as deeply as you. Being the child is different than being the spouse. It is unfair to think they are not grieving; they are." He paused. "In their own way."

Silently, I reminded myself that each of us grieves uniquely...and that each death is unique. I don't know that any of us are fully prepared for the death of a loved one or for the way grief will present itself.

Deciding to shift remembrances, I asked Alan to share with me some of his most vivid memories of Mary. He smiled. "Her gentleness, her kindness, her easy soft laugh. Though a mathematical genius, she was a humble person; she never drew attention to her gifts and talents. She was artistic." He paused, then continued. "She had a calm attitude to life. Her calm, strong faith kept her from having any fear of her illness. She believed that death is like going from one room to another, and she had a very peaceful death."

"From that other room, do you feel you've had contact with Mary?"

"No, not yet, but I expect it may happen. It'd be wonderful, but I'm not holding my breath. It'll happen when it will." Smiling broadly, eyes twinkling, Alan told me, "Eighteen months following my father's death, I had a wonderful experience with him." He did not elaborate; I did not pry.

I asked Alan if there was something he wished I had asked him. He told me I'd not asked about things that might have been a bother or especially painful. "There was something that greatly disturbed me. After Mary died, I received letters and phone calls, lots of them, from Catholic friends who told me they were praying for her soul to leave purgatory soon. That made me angry. In my own effort to be fair, I asked myself if my anger was already there before their calls. I tried to be understanding and tolerant. I felt sorry for them that they thought Mary had to be purged before seeing God. At the time, it was really hard to take. I was angry that friends thought she was in purgatory and not in Heaven. Writing thank-you notes to those friends was very difficult. Thankfully, my offense morphed into sadness for those who doubted Mary's whereabouts." He paused again and added, "All of that came as a surprise."

"There is another thing I've learned," he said. "Books about grief can come too early. In the first six months, they did not help. And, I'd previously read C.S. Lewis' *A Grief Observed*, but after Mary's death it was totally different."

As we were ending our discussion, with a big smile Alan said to me, "I do want to emphasize that, eventually, Christmas was very happy, which was a surprise. The grandchildren had a big part in it."

"When you're asked to speak memories, they become real," Alan said. "It's a privilege to bring them into words."

His privilege is our blessing.

Joe

I thought I could describe a state; make a map of sorrow. Sorrow, however,
turns out to be not a state but a process.
- C.S. Lewis

Seven months plus several days after Bill died, his friend Joe said to me, "I miss him more than all the people I've missed put together. Intense feelings have washed over me in the past few weeks. He was a two-hundred-forty-pound baby; he dwindled to one forty-five. I did everything for him and loved doing it. That was an intimacy like no other." Theirs is a unique story.

A veteran of the U.S. military who had served heroically in several of its branches, Bill spent time in the civilian workforce in Louisiana before moving to a small town on the Alabama coast to be closer to his parents. There, he was employed by a growing real estate firm co-owned by Joe and a partner. Bill became one of their top salesmen. Fate intervened when, in far-south Florida, Bill suffered a major myocardial infarction which resulted in his being in ICU for weeks, then followed by three months in a Florida brain-rehab facility. Bill was diagnosed with anoxic encephalopathy, needing life-long, 24-7, round-the-calendar care. Separately, his Boca Raton- based neurologist and cardiologist had predicted his life expectancy would not exceed six months. Bill lived another 27 years.

Though Bill had lost the ability to talk, to the shock of all involved, that also changed. Following his heart attack, Bill had not spoken for 12 years until one day, seated by the back-yard pool, Bill spied a young man and hollered out, "Get your ass over here." After considerable thought, Joe concluded Bill's returned speaking ability was related to having recently twice treated Bill's Vietnam War-caused PTSD with 5 mg of Valium.

Seeking validation, Joe worked closely with the medical community and the North American Brain Injury Association. A hospice nurse studied the Valium/speech issue and verified its possible relationship to Bill's speaking.

Early in life, because of personal and familial challenges, Joe had become a compassionate problem solver. As hard-working, likable guys, and ignoring the eight-year difference in age, Joe and Bill became friends. When medical personnel predicted Bill had no more than six months to live, Joe volunteered to take charge of his care. Together, they proved the early demise prediction to be incorrect. Bill lived for years, some of them at a medical treatment facility but most of them in Joe's home. To care for Bill, Joe found he needed to hire caregivers. There was always activity and camaraderie. Rather than feeling like an intrusion, Joe learned to delight in the closeness growing among them.

About a month before 77-year-old Bill died, Joe told me, "I know that I am very, very close to losing someone who I've diapered, fed, you name it, for twenty-seven years. And the house is always 'alive' day and night with medical folk, all of whom have become good friends of mine. All will vanish simultaneously, and I fear that greatly."

Ultimately it was late onset Parkinson's that dealt the death blow. The disease struck about five years before death and brought immediate, ever-increasing diminishment of Bill's strength and faculties. Along with the other heinous impairments, it caused his death.

The day after Bill died, Joe texted me, "If you have texted or called, please forgive; I'm not able at this time to make sense."

At one time during Bill's long illness, Joe had told me that he looked forward one day to fulfilling a lifelong dream of being able to spend some time in California. Because I hadn't heard from him in a while, about four months after Bill's death I contacted Joe and inquired about his well-being. He said, "You ask, 'Do I have any plans?' Yes, I plan to not do any plan-making until I am damn good and ready. I am in somewhat of a suspended state right now. Normal, one minute, depressed the next. But not just in and of itself. It takes something to trigger a given memory. This was not so much losing a friend, per se, but like losing a twenty-seven-year-old child whom I had raised from his rising from death.... The intimacy was nothing like simply a friendship and certainly nothing like a marriage, but there was no function in which I was not involved. From teaching him to walk, teaching him to talk, cleaning his nether regions, bathing and dressing him, etc. But enough of that. The degree of improvement was astounding. All of his doctors were transfixed if they had known him in the early years of the injury. He was, perhaps, my Eliza Doolittle."

Later, Joe added, "My LOSS, is/was not just the loss of Bill. I had a staff of three paramedics, two overnight nurses, a speech pathologist, a gym owner, a giant RN and a few others. As if a popped balloon, POOF, they were ALL abruptly gone. A home that usually was 'populated' for many years by three or more INSTANTLY found me alone. I'm not fearful; I'm adrift."

On a different day, reminiscing once again with me, Joe remarked, "We were two males, almost strangers, and one-and-a-half years after meeting, we became much more than that. I took better care of myself because of needing to take care of him. In a sense, we were taking care of each other." He paused, then continued, "I hired a personal trainer for Bill. Now he is mine." Joe has confided in me about memory issues. I call that grief-fog. He does not and has sought medical advice. He is not alone in doing so, and often that is an excellent choice. Though still in emotional pain, Joe has shared some silver linings. "It is so rewarding seeing someone who was not expected to make it live for another twenty-seven years. After getting Bill past the first year, it was educational, spiritual, and wonderful. I learned to love myself through doing for another."

Carol

That which does not kill me makes me stronger.
- Friedrich Nietzsche

Carol has no memories of the day preceding her son Paul's death, yet she vividly remembers the day of the accident. "I was at work," Carol told me, "cleaning my office. I began to cry. I was crying and crying and didn't know why." Her tears came before she was told of his fatal accident.

"And the day after his death," I asked, "do you have memories of that?"

"It was such a blow," she answered. "I can't even tell you anything about that day."

Carol hesitated and began to smile just a little. She was remembering the week before his death. She told me that Paul was living in a city about seventy miles away. He had phoned her saying that he wanted to ride his motorcycle home for a visit and then asked if she'd drive over to pick up a friend and some clothes. He waited for her arrival, was excited she had come to help, and hugged and kissed her, saying, "I love you." Then his friend hugged her. And playfully, her son repeated his hug. They did this laughingly four different times with each of her son's hugs a little more intense.

Her smile faded a little as she said, "I'm so grateful I had that."

Carol's eyes left mine. I waited to hear where her thoughts had taken her. It was obvious to me that nine years after her son's death, she continues to struggle.

Carol turned to look at me. "After Paul's funeral, I was lying down by myself. I asked him for a sign. You may not believe this, but I heard him saying, 'Mom, I'm right here with you. I'll be here every step of the way. This is everything I've

30

been looking for; it's amazing.' And then, Paul added, 'Don't get caught up in religion there; it's all about your relationship with God.'"

"About four days later," Carol continued, "I thought I heard Paul talking to me again. He was explaining what life is all about. He compared life to a tree. It starts with you going straight up, but then sometimes you go out on branches until you return to going straight up...to the path which is to Heaven." And then he told her, "I can see you; I'm still with you."

Carol stopped talking. After waiting a few moments, I asked her about ways her life may have changed since her son's death.

Her immediate reply: "Nothing is the way it used to be. His death has put life into perspective. Things that used to be major are minor now. I realize I've gotten through one-hundred percent of the days since his death. And," she said, "I worry less. God will provide, and God does."

"Does the term grief brain or grief fog mean anything to you?", I asked her.

"Fog, definitely fog!" she said. "Simple words escape me. I'll want an apple and ask for 'that red thing' because I can't remember the word *apple*; things like that. And time escapes me. Sometimes, I want silence. Even now, nine years later, I'll forget what I wanted to do or say. Sometimes, I'll walk into a room and walk out and then back in again, not remembering what I wanted. For sure, grief fog...mine is ongoing. I've learned that there are people twenty-five years out from the death of a loved one who admit they still have it, have fog. And child loss is the most complicated grief." She paused for a moment. "Anger returns. Feelings are all over the place. Sleep is sometimes difficult."

I asked Carol what moves her away from grief. "Nothing," she said. "I learned to live with my grief. It's no longer a new feeling—a part of me now. It's helped," she continued, "to be around others who have lost children. And it helps me to be there for them, too." She hesitated before continuing, "When I hear someone tell me, 'You are so strong,' what I hear them say is that they think I must not have loved my son as much as they loved theirs. The meaning to me is that they couldn't have made it through, couldn't have survived. What they have said hurts. And, they have no awareness that I hurt so badly that I'd been praying, 'God take me!'"

"I began being helped," she continued, "when I learned about a group called Compassionate Friends. I was able to realize that I'm not alone."

Carol pivoted again. "For the first time since months after Paul's death, I could not talk about it. I didn't know how to say it. I had not known that level of pain existed." She paused again, then went on, "Long-time friends wanted the old Carol back; they wanted to fix it, to again do together what we did that we had loved doing. But the old Carol doesn't exist."

Again, she paused. "So, you lose close friends. They don't know how to handle you." Carol hesitated, then added, "God works in crazy, mysterious ways."

We both smiled. I asked about possible additional contact with Paul since his death. She laughed and began telling me about flies slowly crawling on her hand, about seeing lots and lots of flies, and about specific movements of the flies. She laughed. "That's his way of letting me know. Other people see butterflies and cardinals. I get flies. And," she continued, "I also find dollar bills and pennies, lots of pennies. Once, as I was picking up a penny, I heard Paul say, 'I got you, babe.' And then I began finding pennies all the time."

Carol expanded on those thoughts telling me that it helps to open up your eyes and your mind to unique ways a deceased loved one communicates. "It's like learning a new language. It took time for me to know this, to be open, to really feel my feelings, and to experience those things."

After a moment to catch her breath, Carol continued, "I

know now about having a personal relationship with God... not specific beliefs or rituals."

Then, hesitating a moment, Carol shifted a bit, saying, "If somebody wants to hear about your grief, it's like, **OK**, great— let it out!"

I asked Carol if there were other things she wanted to share with me.

"My grief is for my child," Carol said. "Just because he's not here, he's still my child! I still celebrate his birthday with cake. I put balloons on the side of the road where his [fatal] accident occurred. And I find ways and places to say my child's name as a way to honor him. Losing my son," she continued, "has made me a better person. I would do anything to have him back, but his death has made me more compassionate, more helpful to others. I'm not saying I'm grateful—NO! I do know he's in a better place." Hesitating just a moment, she continued, "Paul had a period when he struggled with drugs. He had to work hard not to be led back to that. Maybe God helped him avoid that."

Carol sat quietly for a moment, as did I, before she continued, "I was helped by a group, by Compassionate Friends, but some can't be in a group. It helps, though, to talk about your grief, to release it, or it fills you and festers. You need to talk, to let it out."

David

"The death of a beloved is an amputation."
- C.S. Lewis

What had once been their bed, he slept in alone. She slept nearby in a hospital bed. For the last weeks of her life, around-the-clock nursing aides were also there. Norma was unconscious for the final week. Her death was inevitable, it was just a question of when. At 4 a.m., David was awakened; his wife of 36 years had died.

In the earlier years of Norma's illness, they could and did do some things independently. Theirs was definitely a long good-bye, seven years from diagnosis to death. During Norma's final seven weeks, for 1,176 hours, David left only to get medications or food. He stayed with her. "It seemed like the natural thing to do," he said. "There wasn't a question to do otherwise." Recently retired, David acknowledged that being a physician empowered his tenacity for being with her 24/7 and told me: "There are a variety of hospice personnel constraints. I could manage her increasingly complex medications; she would suffer less."

Then David was still there; bur Norma wasn't. She was gone. Devastation. David was overwhelmed with thoughts of Norma. He could not think of life without her. He took photographs: "My last chance to have views of her." He walked her body to the hearse.

Having told me about his last moments with Norma, David struggled to hold back tears. Years have passed since he could feel her pulse, stroke her hair, smell her essence.

Relating to his emotional memories, I had paused before continuing, before asking him what he remembered, if anything, about grief brain or fog. "You can use those terms interchangeably," he told me. "Grief takes over," he said. "It went on for some time; I don't remember exactly how long." Then he added, "A friend from my hometown called; she called and told me, 'You can get grief amnesia, you know, which luckily passes after a time.' For a while, I couldn't string words together very well and was terribly forgetful. I have also heard it called grief dementia." David struggled again to hold back tears.

"What has helped you move beyond grief fog?"

With little hesitation, David told me that being able to talk to people helped, "especially people," he said, "who would listen to me talk again and again and again about Norma and about our relationship. One of them was a good friend of Norma's." David hesitated, then mentioned well-meaning neighbors who invited him over. He recalled being glad to have the opportunity to be with them, but remembered feeling hurt and anxious when those neighbors avoided even mentioning his wife. "I had to tell them to talk about Norma."

And talk he did...to me. His manner of expression was endearing, that of a gentleman of the "old school." David's face softened as he told me with great enthusiasm, "I remember when we had started to court. And I remember we decided to take a trip to New York together. We went to plays, restaurants, museums. We had a wonderful time. We were there together, but we did not have sexual relations. We were getting to know each other on a deeper level."

He hesitated, again thinking about Norma's final years. "The longer the process of dying is, the more it seems to seep in. Seven years of treatment, but actual death was still a shock. Seven years of treatment—day by day, hour by hour, then minute by minute. The longer the time is, the love gets stronger and stronger."

In a softer voice, David told me of Norma's generous nature. Before her illness had progressed beyond possible conversation, Norma told him she thought he'd marry again. "I told her, 'No.'" And again, I could see tears forming in David's eyes as his demeanor changed to control them.

He reached for a book he had brought with him for me to read: *Living When a Loved One Has Died* by Earl A. Grollman. After Norma's death, a friend had emailed him about the book, recommending he order a copy. David found the sentiments to be "right on" with "just the amount of words needed." Talking about the book seemed to help David steady himself.

David made it clear he does not think grief is a path to be traveled alone. "You need to talk to someone. You just can't keep it within. If you have to cry, cry. You need to tell people; you need an emotional release. Express it —talk, talk. Don't keep it in."

As David's life has continued, music and reading have been helping distractions. He acknowledges he needed to find a new life without Norma. He's joined groups to be with different people in alternative venues and has confided that sometimes that's still an effort.

It has been seven and a half years since Norma died. David misses her. And loves her still.

Jane

*You cannot plant an acorn in the morning and expect
that afternoon to sit in the shade of the oak.*
- Antoine de Saint-Exupery

Her always-engaging smile quickly faded. Jane had come to talk to me about her older sister, Sarah, who had died a few days less than three months earlier and just before what would have been her eighty-sixth birthday. As we talked, I began to realize this would be tough for us both. Our parents had been friends, and we shared both good times and bad throughout our lives.

Jane, tired and somewhat nervous, began our conversation by talking about how much she has going on in her life, how exhausting it all is, adding, "I just have to put that aside." Then she veered to mentioning one of her closest lifelong friends, Lillie, who died six weeks after her sister.

I asked about the 24 hours before her sister Sarah's death. Immediately, she recalled her sister having said to her, "Jane, you know you tick me off sometimes, but I do love you." Jane hesitated just a moment before telling me she thought Sarah may have been trying to be funny. Jane didn't think it was funny, recalling that in the last few years, her sister would often have hurtful flashes of anger.

It was obvious that Jane had returned to Sarah's last day, to the final minutes, as she said, "When you see glassy eyes, you know they're gone." For some moments, I could say nothing.

Mentally, I was searching for Elizabeth Kubler-Ross's terms for our coping mechanisms during and following the terminal illness of a loved one: Denial and Isolation, Anger, Bargaining,

Depression, Acceptance, and ultimately Hope…in no particular order and often randomly felt and exhibited. Jane seemed to have jumped in moments from Anger to Acceptance.

When I asked Jane if she had any particular memories of the 24 hours after Sarah's death, she answered quickly, "No particular thoughts." She looked up a second later adding, "I thought about how to handle it. And, I was concerned about the obituary, how it was being written and if it would be ok."

In the days and weeks afterward, there were a myriad of things to do. And she felt responsibilities to her own children, grandchildren, and even a great-grandchild.

But she no longer needed to regularly visit Sarah. With her signature smile, Jane told me, "Now my car wants automatically to turn toward her house. I have to remind myself there's no need."

Returning to an earlier thought, she added "I feel guilty I couldn't help her overcome her anger." We talked briefly about that anger…things from childhood, lost loves, and parental illnesses and deaths. We recalled her sister's late-life physical limitations and sometimes dogged, even angry, refusal to admit them or to take necessary care.

And what about grief? As we moved toward exploring the experience, Jane told me there'd really been no grief with Sarah. "Some of it is what I believe…." She drifted toward another memory, mentioning again the very long bedridden illness and even more recent death of Lillie, thoughts to which she would continue to return.

"When you see death coming for a long time, it's almost a relief," Jane said. "Then it takes a while to get past all that. Eventually, you start to remember the way they were, and that's easier." She paused. "A friend once told me, 'When death is a shock, the effect on the body is like surgery.'"

In an effort to lighten our mood, I asked about happy memories. I failed to alter the direction of thought. Jane reminisced, "I have more happy memories with Lillie. We were very close friends." She looked away briefly. "I have more grief."

And I thought to myself that the grief was even more recent, grief upon grief.

"There are happy memories," Jane continued. "With Sarah, I have to go back to early life, to Mother and Dad. We had fun as children. I have special memories of playing games in the car when we'd be driving long distances. Our pre-school and grammar school years, we were happy; as teenagers, we began fighting a lot. In her last years Sarah couldn't do a lot." Jane's tone changed. "I had to visit her. She could not come to me. I had to go to her." Grieving aloud, Jane recalled times when Sarah seemed so insecure. Jane smiled tentatively when mentioning Sarah's desire to be glamorous and observing touches of that in her home, things to which she'd paid little attention before her sister's death but could see starkly in the weeks after when she went there to help with what needed to be done.

"For some years, we had a difficult relationship. A difficult relationship makes a difficult grief. Sometimes you are drowning in a situation trying to handle life, one that goes beyond what you know; the good Lord knows," Jane told me. "With Sarah, it was more than I could fix." Jane recollected what seemed to be some dementia, some irrationality. "Sarah did not want to admit she was sick."

Jane mentioned her husband, who had died a few months short of four years before Sarah. "When he died, time stood still."

"With my sister, I'm not aching or crying. I do grasp the reality she's no longer there." Jane reminded me that about five weeks after Sarah's death, a first cousin had died. And about nine days later, her good friend Lillie died. And about two months after that, a close family friend and business associate died. "They all had long lives; they were all over eighty. I have to be thankful for what they had."

"What's helped you cope?" I asked.

"My sweet son who stays in touch; he calls a lot...we're copasetic. And my daughter and her family...I'm lucky to have family here. I go to church; faith is helping."

Jane paused, chuckling: "I wish I had a meter. I have massive highs or lows."

I thought to myself, "This is typical of grief brain's fog."

Another pause, and then Jane continued, "I have a life. Some people don't. I'm not alone. Support of family and friends help the most."

Jane's eye contact with me was on and off. She seemed to be struggling in several ways.

Looking directly at me, however, she said, "Life's difficulties make you more empathetic. It's just life...humanity."

When I asked Jane if she thought she'd had any after-death contact with her sister, she quickly responded, "No." Then, almost as quickly said, "Maybe. Let me modify that. On a spiritual level, I think she's probably there. And I'm so glad she's at peace. She wasn't for so long, and there wasn't anything I could do to fix that for her."

Explaining what she meant, Jane again told me about some of their visits when Sarah was difficult, contentious. There was anger, and Jane would not know its source. "I'm so glad she's at peace now." She paused. "After her divorce, when her kids were young, she used to say I was the only one who supported her." Another pause. "I think she did want me to know she loved me."

She smiled at me. "I think figuring out is part of grief; being scattered is part of grief." Another brief pause. "Or are you trying to figure yourself out? Is that the goal of grief," she asked, "to figure yourself out?"

Melanie

One's suffering disappears when one lets oneself go,
when one yields—even to sadness.
- Antoine de Saint-Exupery

With her usual calmness and good humor, Melanie did not wait for me to begin my inquiry. "I took Valentine's flowers to John's grave yesterday," she said, laughing a little. "There was a huge dog poop on top of his grave and another one to the side." And chuckling a bit louder, she added, "That dog probably did another big one after hearing him 'scream' from the grave."

As I settled into a chair in her home, I asked about the 24 hours before John's death. "Numbness," she said. "He was in intensive care. I was just going through the motions." At the hospital where he had been for a week, sitting near him, she would talk aloud to him, not with any certainty he could hear her but with awareness that his death was imminent. "I'd tell him that I would be ok and that he would be ok, too." She recalled being by his bed when he died, though saying she was not certain of the exact moment, the designated time of death.

As to the 24 hours following John's death, Melanie said, "About the same as the twenty-four hours before. I knew it was coming. I was like a robot. You know, you just don't want to allow yourself to think. I knew that life would be totally changed. I was praying that God would give me strength." She paused, then continued, "He was taken off all life support. I can't remember little details; they were drowned out by the situation."

When a nurse confirmed his death, Melanie says she felt a sense of acceptance, of relief. "I was grateful it was over and

41

he was not in pain." She continued, "I don't mind being by myself. I'm ok being alone. I'm happy reading, talking to others by phone or text. I can entertain myself without others." She paused. "I missed him. That was counteracted by gratefulness that he did not suffer, that he had not lingered longer. At his age, death was the natural way of life; he left me well cared for. There was a foggy period. I remember feeling grateful that John had not been the one to be left alone. He would have been miserable. He was so active. He was larger than life. He wanted to be with others. He had so many interests and commitments to family and to the community. God gave me the gift of being the kind of person I am. I could manage better alone, so He took John first so that he wouldn't have to."

After John's death, Melanie recalled activity, lots of activity. "There were so many distractions. There were so many family and friends here. He's gone. That was more of a fact. He was here; within two weeks and two days, he was not. I was on automatic pilot. I wasn't in charge of anything. I would do what others told me to do. I went through the motions. I didn't feel much of anything. I think I felt more fog related to the added responsibilities of being alone than to his death. I was fortunate I had family here." Chuckling a little, she added, "There was all the business that needed attending." She said she'd reminded herself she was lucky to have had him as long as she did and, again, that he was spared extended pain. "Rather than being emotionally bereft, I'm more grateful." And she described the tasks that each of her three sons had assumed, relieving her of the necessity. They continue to help.

As I continued to make notes of our conversation, Melanie volunteered, "What surprises me was John's reaction to his fatal diagnosis." She veered to tell me, "My heart dropped to the floor when his doctor told me, 'We're not going to talk about how much time he has.'"

Following that, she said, "John never looked at me or the children. He stared at a wall. His attitude changed. He never mentioned it and gradually pulled away; emotional intimacy was gone."

I felt her pain and his. I cried. Saying goodbye after almost sixty years of marriage, of ups and downs, of being there for each other...how does one do that? How does one hold it together for the great goodbye?

Looking at my notes, I asked if she still experiences any grief fog.

"It's gone now. I think that's because I was so accepting of his death because the alternative would have been so terrible for him...not cure but a long, lingering illness." She attributed her ability to move beyond the fog to his short illness, telling me, "He went quickly, and I'm the kind of person who can live alone. And," she added, "John had a long productive life and was spared a lengthy painful death."

"What do you remember most vividly about him now?" I asked.

"He was loud." She softly chuckled, "And I'm not. I did not like that. He was in charge; he could do anything he set his mind to do. He was honorable, of the highest integrity and character—a good man. He could be short-tempered. He was careful with money but very generous."

She paused for a minute and confided that since his death, on occasion, she had asked him as though he was still here, still in body, about tending to the work persons she needed for keeping the house and yard in good repair. She laughed, saying she'd had no reply.

As we were finishing our conversation, Melanie mentioned her mother-in-law, whose husband was 63 when he died. Widowed at the age of 57, "she was a lesson for anybody; at such a young age, she accepted and went on. John's death was the natural order of things."

Ryan

Grief is like a long valley, a winding valley where
any bend may reveal a totally new landscape.
- C.S. Lewis

It has been thirty-four years and three months since Gloria's death just a few months before her forty-eighth birthday. Her husband, Ryan, is still living and agreed to talk to me. Frankly, I was hoping he would tell me that passing years help loss and painful memories diminish. I asked the same questions I had asked of everyone.

In the 24 hours leading up to Gloria's death, Ryan recalled, she continued to sleep on her side of their shared bed in their bedroom at home.

"You were actually able to continue sleeping with her?" I asked.

He hesitated for just seconds, explaining, "Being there by her, I could check on her breathing and pain level, and I could press a button for her morphine line if necessary. Only in the last few days did she have difficulty with breathing. Prior to that, Gloria could sit in a wheel chair and be able to walk around some."

Taking a moment to search his memory, Ryan continued, "During those last days, her parents had come to live with us in our home. They wanted to be with their daughter when she died, and we all wanted that." He paused, chuckling as he continued, "Her dad was an assertive, controlling type, and when Gloria died, he wanted to take over, to make the important decisions. He began telling me who to call and why. He argued a bit and harrumphed a bit when I did things my way. But he was there, and that was the important thing." After a brief pause, Ryan told me that their older daughter, Gwen, had just finished college and had been in the first week or ten days of a new job in another city. "When we suspected Gloria had only minutes to live, we called Gwen and put the phone to her mother's ear so that Gwen could speak to her. That was good for Gwen, and it was good closure for all of us. Gloria died a few minutes later."

I asked Ryan what he remembered about the first 24 hours after she died. Interestingly, I saw the same vacant look that I had seen in others whose loved ones had died more recently. When he spoke, he said, "I know I had some important matters to care for. I remember, as a family, we were calling friends and relatives. We needed to notify the church, decide arrangements with the funeral home, and contact the newspaper. I don't remember who in the family did what. I do remember the ambulance coming to pick up Gwen's body. I walked out with her body, at least I think so, probably because I remember seeing neighbors looking on."

Gloria had been ill for several years. They had gone to special clinics, first in Texas and then in Tennessee. The final visit was when they had to accept a terminal diagnosis. Gloria wrote in her diary: "We have to let it run its course; what horrible words."

"For the last month and a half before she died," Ryan told me, "our life had been almost the same. Gloria was very functional until the last weeks."

"And after her death?" I asked.

"After the details were done, the funeral over, then I got a first sense of aloneness; I guess a different stage. Our younger daughter, Betsy, was still living at home while she was finishing college and was a big help. But I had to accept the reality of a different life: alone, solitary." Again, Ryan paused, remembering. "I had to cook, to handle all the bills, tend to all the details. I had duties, responsibilities, but it felt so solitary." He paused, then continued, "I missed Gloria's presence, her voice, her familiar footsteps on the back porch, and surely her companionship."

For me, I could feel what he meant. I had known Gloria as a fun-loving, vivacious person with a singular laugh that always pulled others into her sense of mirth. Ryan's solitude was a natural by-product of her absence.

Again, I sat quietly as Ryan seemed to be remembering more and collecting his thoughts. "The fact that I was working at the time was a huge help. But on the weekends, there was no getting dressed or going out, just the awkwardness of feeling alone," he said.

"Do you think you experienced brain fog, that grieving made thinking foggy?" I asked. Without hesitation, Ryan said, "I had fog preparing for work. I can remember walking into work and thinking, 'What the hell am I going to do today?'"

"But having a job, going to work," he said, "was a lifesaver. Work was a necessary distraction. And when I had out-of-town work, that was a wonderful escape...getting away from town, from an empty house. As time went by, my friends and daughters were a big help. Being active, especially participation in tennis and golf groups, was a huge escape."

Ryan recalled that selling his wife's car was difficult, discomforting. "Going to the cemetery helped," he said. "I had a feeling of closeness being there."

In the early years after Gloria's death, Ryan told me that he sought activities to keep himself busy, things to keep him away from his loss and sorrow. "Even cutting the grass or working in the yard helped. Often I would feel the need to get out of the house, like going shopping or just walking through a mall. At night, when I left home, I'd leave lights turned on in the house with the TV on to welcome me back. A few times I even called my home phone and left messages so that when I came into the house, the light on the phone would be blinking."

Sometimes, while listening to Ryan, I had to remind myself

that his wife had died more than thirty-four years ago. I asked him if or when things had begun to change.

"As time moved on," he said, "I started having more acceptance. For a year or more after Gloria died, I kept her greeting on our phone's voice-message system. I stopped wearing my wedding ring about two years after she died.

"And two to three years after Gloria's death," he continued, "I attended a retreat called the Beginning Experience. It was about understanding grief, but in a social setting. I think it was a signal that I was ready to move on. There would be brief talks about trust or personal guilt or other things, and then we'd break into small discussion groups. You'd write about yourself and then move into small groups to share. The course culminated with each individual writing a letter to their departed loved one. I felt that retreat was very insightful and helped me a lot. Eventually, I became a facilitator rather than a participant."

As with others I had interviewed, I asked Ryan what he most remembers about Gloria. He quickly replied, "Her zest, her enthusiasm, her laugh, quick wit, and personality. She was very sensitive, caring, and was very giving. She was warm and made friends easily. And she made decisions based on facts. She could be tough, especially if someone wronged one of the kids.

When I asked Ryan if he thought he may have had contact with Gloria since she died, he told me he had had dreams about her. He'd even had some in the past few months, more than thirty years after her death.

"Do you think there's anything she'd want for you now?" I asked.

Ryan thought a few moments before saying, "For my health to be better. And, probably she'd want me to have an enjoyable relationship."

Having said that, Ryan returned to talking about memories. "I remember our trips and travel with our girls and with extended family, often in Florida or North Carolina. After Gloria's death, we continued our trips to North Carolina, which we continue to take almost annually. It's as though her presence accompanies us. We often talk about her and what she would have thought about various things."

Ryan seemed to be looking past me into some warm, personal, nearby recollection. "I remember her style," he said, "the way she dressed and acted socially. She smiled a lot and was very animated." His facial expression was one of appreciation, of love.

PART TWO

POSSIBLE PATHS TO A BRIGHTER BEYOND

Accepting

Though life changed in an instant, you can expect it to take time to grasp all that it means. Probably, it will be trial and error; start and stop. There's no one way to integrate the loss of a friend or loved one into daily living.

Start with memories. Remind yourself especially of those things that made you happy, and allow yourself to smile at the memories. Let the smile bubble into a giggle or hearty laugh.

You may want to write a note to your loved one who has died, say things you wished you had but hadn't. You can speak those thoughts. Either way, know that you are heard.

Remind yourself of things they liked to do. Choose one and give it a try. If you don't want to do this alone, find another family member or mutual friend to do it with you. For example, you might travel to a favorite place, volunteer with an admired charity, or eat a favorite food.

Remember the basics: eat, sleep, and exercise regularly.

Be open to new possibilities —entertainment, volunteer organizations, hobbies, people. Ask others about bereavement groups. Choose one; attend. An organization called Heartmath (heartmath.com) has conducted studies that indicate care and compassion for each other increase "the heart energy or love" that flows through our system, helping us to restore emotional balance.

On days when you do not feel like talking to anyone, write a note to someone you love or admire, or to a person who has been especially kind to you. You can mail the note, email it, or text it. A kindness toward someone else is also a kindness to yourself.

If today you can do none of these things, try again tomorrow and again the next day until you can do one of them.

When you are ready, do another one. You're like the favorite childhood story *The Little Engine that Could:* "I think I can, I think I can—and did." "I thought I could, I thought I could, I thought I could."

If you seem stalled, however, if for months you continue to be depressed or preoccupied with thoughts of your loved one, find a professional who offers effective treatment. Make an appointment. Arrive on time.

Relieving Stress

Grief and stress accompany loss. It's virtually inevitable. Admittedly, when you are deeply grieving, it's hard to do almost everything.

Most of us need and want relief. Though it may be difficult to get yourself to do anything, it's worth the effort.

There are a variety of stress reducers. Some of the following may work for you. Why not give one or more a try?

Active possibilities:

- Go for a walk outside

- Ride a bike

- Exercise alone or exercise in a group to be with others

- Stretch

- Yawn

- Play with your pet; if you don't have one, play with your neighbor's

Less active possibilities:

- Enjoy a hobby of your choosing

- Read a good book

- Solve word puzzles

- Complete a jigsaw puzzle

Personal care possibilities:

- Prepare a healthy meal; minimize processed foods
- Be cautious in your use of phone and screen time
- Allow yourself a good cry
- Take a leisurely bath or long shower
- Light candles
- Use a diffuser with calming scents such as lavender, bergamot, or sandalwood
- Get a massage
- Take a nap
- Practice deep breathing
- Chew gum
- Give someone a hug
- Laugh out loud; giggle

Interpersonal possibilities:

- Call a family member or a friend
- Invite a neighbor to visit
- Attend a meeting, a class, or a religious service

Connecting

Do you think you may have interacted with friends, loved ones, and others who are no longer in physical bodies? As possible evidentiary information, friends and acquaintances have told me their personal stories. I have my own. I admit, however, that such experiences can be both satisfying and frustrating.

The first time I think that I heard from my husband was within a few weeks of his death. I sensed his presence so strongly that I turned my head toward the direction of that sensation. When he was not there, I began sobbing, the reality of his absence hitting hard. A few minutes later, an overhead light flashed off and on again, and again, and then again before returning to steady, stable light. Such a strong signal, electric sign language, had not happened before, nor has it happened since.

It is quite possible that your loved ones have tried to alert you of their presence, have tried to let you know that they are with you still and that they care. How might you know? There are many possibilities:

You may, as I did, have lights flicker or have other problems with electric things.

And, as I did, you may sense that someone is with you, that you're not alone in a room. You may feel that someone is sitting or lying beside you when no one is physically present.

You may find coins or have them appear in unusual places. After her husband's death, my sister regularly found coins, especially on long walks she took to ease her grief. And since her death, her grandson has found coins.

You may have unusual experiences with birds or with butterflies. I have had both.

You may look for something in its usual place and find it moved. A friend of my mother's had that happen and asked me to help. As she was describing the missing item belonging to her deceased mother, I saw a picture of it in my mind and shared that vision. She recognized the location and connected with her mother and the item.

One friend of mine frequently smelled her deceased husband's favorite after-shave. Be aware of odors you associate with the deceased, especially when you can't find another source of that smell. That is another way our departed loved ones sometimes connect.

You may experience physical sensations, perhaps like someone is touching you when no one is there. You could experience an unusual tingling sensation or that someone is playfully tickling you. After her husband had died, a friend of mine was awakened one night by her cat stroking her hair in the exact manner of her deceased husband; she accepted that as communication from him.

Numerous people have told me that as they were thinking about a deceased loved one, they'd hear a special song on the TV or radio. The impact would be even greater when it was a song not frequently played on public media outlets.

If you have had a uniquely personal way of communicating with your loved one in life, you may experience some reflection of that.

If it is a special day, loved ones may try to communicate with you. They may use any of the above possibilities or perhaps other more creative ones.

There is no guarantee communication will occur. However, if you think you haven't communicated in any way and want to do so, here are some suggestions:

Pay attention to your dreams. Communication may be easier then. Honestly, sometimes this works for me and sometimes not. Sometimes, I cannot remember any dreams. And sometimes, the dream is not from the person I had hoped for or expected; but even that can be wonderful and can be affirmation that communication through dreams is possible. An example since my husband's death is a dream visit from two former neighbors. Though they had died years apart, together they came to me as I was dreaming and asked me to call their older daughter. They were so insistent that I awakened myself, found my iPad and began searching for a phone number. Failing to find one, the next morning I texted a few people and succeeded. The departed, no-longer-in-physical-body friends were concerned with good reason. When I contacted the older daughter, she explained that the afternoon of that night's concerned during-dream visit, her younger sister had fallen and been taken to a hospital emergency room. She assured me proper care had been administered. The call also affirmed the veracity of the dream visit. Perhaps even better, it re-established contact, and I have now been sent pictures of recently birthed twins born to the couple's great-granddaughter. How much fun is that?!

Keep a photo or multiple photos nearby. Photographs bring physical essence to mind and may strengthen your inner-communications. One friend of mine told me how that happened to her. In her den, she has pictures of family members. While seated there one day, missing and thinking about her deceased mother, she heard a crash. Without discernible provocation, a framed picture of her mom had fallen to the floor.

Family members or friends may be able to share their dreams or other possible contacts. They may be hesitant to mention them, afraid perhaps of upsetting you. Ask. Though you may, of course, prefer first-hand communication, hearing through someone else can be satisfying.

Be open to visits from deceased pets who want to comfort you. Twice in the early months after my husband's death, a wonderfully loving dog who had been part of our family forty or so years ago came to me in dreams to let me know she was with my husband, loving him as she had done so many years ago. Her dream visit was a warm surprise.

Some people find it comforting to hold an object that had belonged to a deceased loved one because it retains his vibration, and that may facilitate communication. Scientists disagree about the possibility of a personal vibration. I can attest to something happening.

Years ago, a friend brought a shirt to me to hold, one that had belonged to her deceased son. She badly wanted to hear from him following his accidental death. I held the shirt, relaxed, and almost immediately began seeing mental pictures and getting some clear wording that soothed her. Most strikingly, however, were the things that had no meaning for her. From the notes she had taken as we talked, she later told her daughter about our conversation. The daughter was able to explain what her mom had not understood.

I wrote about another incident in an earlier book: not many weeks after a friend's daughter was killed in an accident, she dislodged a meaningful book in my home during the night and somehow placed it in my pathway from my bedroom to the kitchen for me to find as I went to pour my morning coffee.

Watch for birds or butterflies behaving in unusual ways. As a younger cousin was dying, I asked her how I would know she was ok. She told me to watch for the butterflies. At her burial, an amazingly large swarm of yellow butterflies flew among us. A friend told me of sitting in his den, allowing himself to fully experience the loss of someone he greatly admired. Through his tears, he looked out the window to his back yard, where an extremely unusual number of cardinals were perched in his trees. While seated outside, following the deaths of my husband and sister, I had two hummingbirds fly to within ten inches of my face and hover for almost a minute; years before, I had a similar experience following the deaths of two close friends.

You can ask your loved ones to make their presence known...think it, but also say it out loud. Be open to responses whether words, odors, physical changes, music, an unusual noise, or other unique communication possibilities.

Unfortunately, there are no guarantees. If you are open to the possibility that your loved one can communicate with you, the more likely you may recognize it's happening. Hold the hope.

Blending the New
With the Old

Death is loss. Some learn, as I did, that losing a loved one can be excruciatingly painful. Everything about the future seems uncertain. You learn that it hurts to love. You feel different inside your own skin. You are more fragile. You experience changes. In one reported case, following her husband's death, a woman went to bed for two years before venturing slowly out into the world of daily tasks and human contact. I don't recommend that.

You may be filled with longing for what no longer is, a return to what cannot be. Like stress and depression, yearning is also characteristic of grief.

For some, grieving may result in interrupted sleep, fatigue, depression, increased anxiety, or scattered thinking. It's even possible for your immune system to be jeopardized. I believe that happened to me when, in two separate instances, I had complications with minor skin cancer removal surgeries. And, as the surviving lonely spouse, your death could be hastened, especially if you allow yourself to be socially isolated. Just what does hastened mean? That seems to depend on many individual variables.

You are aware of your loneliness. Loss hurts. Some fear it. Emily Dickinson has called it "the horror not to be surveyed" with "consciousness suspended."

It isn't enough to have your loss and loneliness recognized. You need to find a way to lessen it, to fully live again. What do you do?

One path is pushing yourself to be with people again.

Though that is good, often it isn't enough. You need cama-raderie, but even more so, you may need a sense of purpose. When you can make something meaningful happen for oth-ers, your own well-being improves.

Combining your need to be with others and the benefits of helping can result in personal improvements; there seems to be a win-win benefit to doing for others while enjoying a sense of community. You don't have to initiate a group; you can join an existing one. Volunteers are welcomed and appre-ciated. What are your interests? Offer help to a group in what-ever ways you can. If you still feel too numb, ask a friend or family member to help you get started or perhaps volunteer with you.

Though the grieving process is a natural thing, it some-times feels like a sledgehammer that hits without warning. Ending grief fog may take painful effort and determination. You may need help. That's ok. A Biblical recommendation offers a possibility, one that requires you to do more than think about taking your own steps to move ahead: "Ask and it will be given to you; seek and you will find; knock and the door will be opened to you." (Matthew 7:7). In other words, speak up; say something to somebody. It doesn't have to be a major undertaking; something simple will do. Try calling a friend or family member. I'd say text or send an email, but that isn't enough. You need to hear a voice, and to have yours heard. Something simple is good enough, like, "Hi, I haven't talked to you in a while and wanted to hear your voice. How are you?" And with that question, you don't have to talk any-more until it's your turn to answer a question or initiate a comment.

An amusing way for some is to get a group together to share stories of strange things they have done because of grief. Causes of grief-induced, unusual behaviors can result in head-shaking, can-you-believe-that laughter. You help each other move away from inaction to possibility, taking baby steps toward the new life that you begin to create. If you are like me, you may be thinking "But I don't want a new life; I want to continue the one I had." Someone in your gathering can help you take a step toward new.

And, if you're at all like I have been, there'll be times you don't want to be with others. Instead of sulking or wallowing in your sadness, use your memories of happy times at whatever age or stage of your life. Watch mental movies of fun times in your past. What were your hobbies? Enjoy those reflections and then use them! Were you doing things then that you can do now? If you need to write them down, if grief fog might obliterate those memories, then do make notes! Later, with notes in hand, decide which of those things you can do now. Maybe you want to build a model airplane, paint with watercolors, or plant a vegetable garden. Have fun using the younger you to pattern a going forward you.

"Are you following your own advice?" you might ask. Yes, I am. Though I do not consider myself to be a professional writer, I've previously published books and articles. Moving in and out of grief fog, I've used my computer and the written word to do two things: to recognize my feelings and to connect me to others.

Do what you can. And, for heaven's sake, don't beat up on yourself if going forward is bumpy and twisty. Just keep going forward, away from the fog. I keep reminding myself of that.

Angels

Living in the United States of America, it is almost impossible to avoid hearing about angels. Beginning sometime in November and throughout December, Christmas songs are played through loudspeakers in stores and sometimes on street corners; we hear "Hark the Herald Angels Sing" and "Angels We Have Heard on High." Angel songs are common. There are popular songs such as "Angels," "Angels Among Us" and "Calling All Angels." And there are hymns heard in churches, including: "Oh, Come Angel Band," "Angels Watching Over Me," and "May the Choirs of Angels (Song of Farewell)." Angel songs have been publicly played all my life...heard but not always registering in my consciousness.

So, had anyone asked me before my husband's death if I would be writing about angels, I'd have smiled curiously and struggled to find words for a polite "no." But that was before I had a prescient email from my brother.

Early in the afternoon of February 3, 2023, I opened my brother's email message. Knowing of my experiences in communicating with people who are no longer in physical bodies (are dead) and of my interest in existence beyond physical life, my brother was forwarding a message he'd received: an unsolicited book recommendation. He added a note saying. "I think this was meant for you. If you want a copy, I'll order it for you."

I clicked on the internet link he had sent, read about the book, and instantly ordered a copy of *Angels in My Hair, The True Story of a Modern-Day Irish Mystic*. Then, I responded to my brother and thanked him, telling him there was no need for him to order for me because I had immediately done so and expected the book would be delivered in a few days.

Hours later in the day, after ordering that angel book, my husband went by emergency transport to the hospital. A few days later, in the hospital, my husband died.

Several days after my husband's unexpected death, the angel book arrived. It was the only thing I could read. Though I cannot recall specifically how it helped, I know it did. And I ordered other books by its author, Lorna Byrne. After repeatedly reading hers, I bought more angel books by other authors.

I read that each of us has a guardian angel, one that is with us for eternity. I read that there are other kinds of angels. Some are helpers for specific goals or reasons. They can work as teams. They are not human nor are they to be human; they are another of God's creations.

And, several of the books I read commented on the many references to angels in the Old and New Testaments used in the Jewish and Christian faiths. I do not remember references to angels in other faiths, such as in Islam, but perhaps there were some.

For me, the companionship of angels revealed through my extensive reading has been a reminder that God works in mysterious ways, my way of expressing belief in a spirituality of existence that exceeds human understanding. I am unsure why it took the death of my husband to unleash my learning about and outreach to angelic beings.

From childhood, I participated in Judeo-Christian studies and worship. As an adult, I also participated in Native North American and Mayan worship rituals. I was honored to have the opportunity to do so.

But angels? Were they there but unrecognized? They were there. I remember one particular instance as an adult when I was in a small prayer circle. There were only about four, maybe five, of us in a circle facing each other, with arms stretched behind each other's backs, pulled in together as tightly as we could. We were concluding a meeting and decided to end it with a prayer of gratitude; I've forgotten why or what that meeting was about. We were silently expressing our gratitude. I remember feeling a powerful strength in the center of our circle, opening my eyes, and seeing a misty form reaching from the floor upward toward the ceiling. I knew the form had essence and meaning; I knew it affirmed our gratitude. I thought then, and still do, that an angel was with our group.

And now? Now, I often speak to "my" angels. I am thankful they contacted me through my brother. I continue to seek more knowledge about them and experiences with them. I anticipate the relationship with angels to continue when I am no longer in my physical body.

And it pleases me to contemplate the ways angels continue helping my loved ones who have left their bodies...especially my husband and sister, whose recent deaths spur my writing.

If the sharing of my angel experiences with you resonates in any way, I urge you to explore your connection or relationship with angels. You have nothing to lose and a lot to gain. Have fun!

A Taste of Honey

It was midday. I was tired. I needed a break from writing. I needed a nap.

With my eyes closed, lying on my bed, drifting into sleep, I heard a voice:

"Turn hardship into honey."

When I awakened about an hour later, I heard the phrase again, "Turn hardship into honey."

With my curiosity aroused, I began looking for the reasons why, for the qualities of honey. I share some with you now:

Honey

- is rich in nutrients and antioxidants,
- has antibacterial properties,
- helps with wound healing and treatment,
- provides an energy boost,
- promotes sleep, and
- helps with heart health and healing.

"Turn hardship into honey."

I hope this book has been a taste of honey for you.

Additional Reading

Elizabeth Kubler-Ross, MD
On Death and Dying
On Life After Death

Raymond Moody, MD with Paul Perry
Reunions, Visionary Encounters with Departed Loved Ones

Pamela M. Kircher, MD
Love is the Link: A Hospice Doctor Shares her Experience of Near-Death and Dying

Morris Weiss, Jr., MD, FACP, FACC
Darwin's Heart

Dillard, Sherrie
I'm Still with You: Communicate, Heal, & Evolve with Your Loved One on the Other Side

P.M.H. Atwater, L.H.D.
The Forever Angels, Near-Death Experiences in Childhood and Their Lifelong Impact
Edge Walker, The Many Lives and Deaths of P.M.H. Atwater

Jim B. Tucker, MD
BEFORE, Children's Memories of Previous Lives

Jeffrey Mishlove, PhD
New Thinking Allowed Dialogues: Is There Life After Death

Stafford Betty

When did you ever become less by dying? Afterlife: The Evidence

Lorna Byrne

Angels in My Hair: The True Story of a Modern-Day Irish Mystic

Lynn B. Robinson, PhD

Coming Out of Your Psychic Closet, How to Unlock Your Naturally Intuitive Self
Loving to the End...and On, A Guide to the Impossibly Possible.

Afterword

Hopefully, reading *Grief Fog* has helped you understand the effects of deep feelings of loss when a loved one dies. Perhaps, also, you've been assisted in recognizing communication with those who are no longer with you in physical bodies.

It is possible to go deeper. For most of my life, I've experienced spontaneous knowings and also interactions with friends and family members who have died. I've written two earlier books with information about that. I've had friends and friends of those friends seek me out to share experiences they were too emotionally or intellectually timid to share with family, colleagues, or other friends. Perhaps you've had similar experiences of the spirit or would like to do so.

In my early adult explorations, I attended several residential programs at the Monroe Institute where the phrase "you are more than a physical body" is often repeated. Begun by businessman Robert Monroe, the Institute offers research and workshops for the exploration of "out-of-body experience" along with practical methods of attaining and using expanded consciousness.

The International Association of Near-Death Studies is "devoted to the study of near-death and similar experiences and their relationship to human consciousness." Though I'm not a near-death experiencer, from 2002 to 2019 I facilitated a local monthly IANDS gathering. I did so because of my experience communicating with those no longer in physical bodies. Especially in the earlier years of our meetings, I knew anyone who attended needed support and validation, something that has since become widespread.

For many years, I was privileged to be a board member of the Intuition Network: "The purpose of the Intuition Network is to help create a world in which all people feel encouraged to cultivate and use their inner, intuitive resources." Board members explored beyond basic intuition into the meaning of consciousness, the probability of reincarnation, and the expectation of life beyond life. Among the amazing people who served on that board were a physician, a world-class professional medium, a psychologist, a renowned artist, and a brilliant serial entrepreneur whose successes bred success for others. Wes Agor, PhD, a professor of management in Texas, initiated and chaired the Network until he passed leadership to Jeffrey Mishlove, PhD, who earned the only doctorate in parapsychology ever awarded in the state of California.

In 2021, Jeff's essay, "Beyond the Brain, The Survival of Human Consciousness After Permanent Bodily Death" was first among three awards from Bigelow Institute's $1.8 million afterlife essay competition. His essay can be read online (https://www.bigelowinstitute.org/docs/1st.pdf) and includes video moments from his YouTube interviews regarding near-death experiences, reincarnation/past life memories, and other evidential offerings of consciousness surviving physical death. By using the video links, you will hear, see, and sense more meaning than by simply reading the written words. As you enjoy those links, explore the ways you may feel more deeply connected to those you love.

Embrace moments of lifted fog.

Be open to contact from those for whom you grieve.

Love and be loved in the here, now, and beyond your physical body.

I appreciate you.

Gratitude

"Grief never ends....but it changes. It's a passage, not a place to stay. Grief is not a sign of weakness nor a lack of faith...it is the price of love."
- Author unknown

This book would not have been written without the life—and death—of Robbie, to whom I dedicate this book.

The love of my family has sustained me: Jennifer and Ann; Ken, Loraine, Jack, Kathleen, and Susan. The love of my brother, Milton; his wife, Margaret; and my sister, Phyllis, along with their children and grandchildren: Samuel, Margaret, Sam, Philip, Leigh, Emily Kate, Samuel, and Jennifer who have added support.

The brave caring folks who agreed to tell their stories are amazing. Without them, there would be no book. Thank you, each one of you.

Friends (both living and deceased) have supported me and encouraged me: Suey, Joan, Kay, Paul, Venetia, Barbara, Marion, Ansley, Judy, Betty, Virginia, Carolyn, Sherrell, Nancy, Sue, Amanda, Sheila, Jeannie, Louise, Sherrie, Bill, Joe, Holly.

Those who read and were willing to write comments are treasures! Thank you Bob, Morris, Sherrill, and Chris.

The professional help I was given by the team at Atmosphere Press, especially by Alex Kale, has made the publication of this book possible. Thank you.

About Atmosphere Press

Founded in 2015, Atmosphere Press was built on principles of Honesty, Transparency, Professionalism, Kindness, and Making Your Book Awesome. As an ethical and author-friendly hybrid press, we stay true to that founding mission today.

Always feel free to visit Atmosphere Press and our authors online at atmospherepress.com. See you there soon!

About the Author

LYNN B. ROBINSON, PHD, is a widow, mother, grand-mother, author, professor emerita of marketing, former business consultant, speaker, and volunteer in numerous non-profit organizations. Her personal experience with grief fog has allowed her to write with insight, sensitivity, and occasional humor.

Made in the USA
Columbia, SC
23 August 2025

61684737R00050